BE REAL IN A FA...

THE BEAUTIFUL

TRUTH

DARE TO BE DIFFERENT I WANT TO MAKE AN IMPACT WHY FIT IN WHEN YOU WERE BORN TO STAND OUT? NO ONE IS ALL BAD

YOU WERE BORN AN ORIGINAL YOU DON'T SEE THE REAL ME I HIDE BEHIND. HEAR ME ROAR BECAUSE THE CURIOUS KEEP TRYING BEAUTY COMES IN ALL SHAPES AND SIZES

GOOD VIBES ONLY RULES ARE MEANT TO BE BROKEN CREATE YOUR OWN DESTINY BITE BACK BEAUTY BEGINS THE MOMENT YOU DECIDE TO BE YOURSELF

REBELLIOUS SPIRITS IGNITE REVOLUTIONS THE TRUTH IS COMPLICATED BE THE CHANGE YOU WISH TO SEE IN THE WORLD BE YOURSELF AN ORIGINAL IS ALWAYS WORTH MORE THAN A COPY A LITTLE REBELLION NOW AND THEN IS A GOOD CHANGE THING YOU

BE YOURSELF EVERYONE ELSE IS TAKEN BE ORIGINAL YOU WERE BORN AN ORIGINAL SPEAK OUT I SEE THE BEAUTY IN OTHERS IF IT DOESN'T CHALLENGE YOU IT WON'T

NEVER DOUBT YOURSELF NOBODY IS PERFECT FOLLOW YOUR DREAMS TAKE THE RISK IF YOU CAN DREAM IT YOU CAN DO IT YOU ARE ENOUGH

IT'S OKAY NOT TO BE OKAY BELIEVE IT AND ACHIEVE IT THIS IS ME BE TRUE TO YOURSELF

GIVE ME TRUTH NEVER GIVE UP

BE BRAVE DREAM BIG YOUR OPINION MATTERS DREAM CREATE INSPIRE WHAT IS YOUR TRUTH? MAKE US UNDERSTAND THE TRUTH MATTERS EXPRESS YOURSELF

MAKE THAT CHANGE

Edited By Lynsey Evans

First published in Great Britain in 2025 by:

Young Writers
Remus House
Coltsfoot Drive
Peterborough
PE2 9BF
Telephone: 01733 890066
Website: www.youngwriters.co.uk

Book Design by Ashley Janson
Softback ISBN 978-1-83685-208-7
Printed and bound in the UK by BookPrintingUK
Website: www.bookprintinguk.com
YB0627R

Foreword

Since 1991, here at Young Writers we have celebrated the awesome power of creative writing, especially in young adults where it can serve as a vital method of expressing their emotions and views about the world around them. In every poem we see the effort and thought that each student published in this book has put into their work and by creating this anthology we hope to encourage them further with the ultimate goal of sparking a life-long love of writing.

Our latest competition for secondary school students, The Beautiful Truth, asked young writers to consider what their truth is, what's important to them, and how to express that using the power of words. We wanted to give them a voice, the chance to express themselves freely and honestly, something which is so important for these young adults to feel confident and listened to. They could give an opinion, highlight an issue, consider a dilemma, impart advice or simply write about something they love. There were no restrictions on style or subject so you will find an anthology brimming with a variety of poetic styles and topics. We hope you find it as absorbing as we have.

We encourage young writers to express themselves and address subjects that matter to them, which sometimes means writing about sensitive or contentious topics. If you have been affected by any issues raised in this book, details on where to find help can be found at
www.youngwriters.co.uk/info/other/contact-lines

Contents

Belle Goulden (12) 78
Everleigh Laing (12) 79

Haywards Heath College, Haywards Heath

Lisa Jarrett 80
Annie Ghag 82
Nelly Pandey 83

Honley High School, Honley

Lillie-Mae Gill (14) 85
Jess Gledhill (14) 86
Isabella-Rose Dent (13) 87
Aniela Szewczyk (13) 88

HSDC, Havant

Grace Jones-Parker (17) 89

Llangatwg Community School, Cadoxton

Erin Osmond (12) 93
Kali Davies (12) 94
Alexander Rowland (14) 96
Savannah Davies (12) 98
Jasmine Evans (14) 99
Lily Crumb (12) 100
Evie Hawkes (11) 101
Grace Williams (13) 102
Olivia Harris (12) 103
Tilly Roach (12) 104
Gwen Hart (13) 105
Lacey Jones (13) 106
Amelia Higgins (12) 107
Lilly-Haf Church (11) 108
Evan Coleman (12) 109
Catalin Lazar (11) 110
Aaron Joseph Case (12) 111
Noah Bradley (12) 112
Reese O'Neale (12) 113
Florence Matthew (13) 114
Adam Griffiths 115

Sophie Roderick (12) 116
Sonny Jon Phillips (12) 117
Lexi Dale (12) 118
Mason Hughes (12) 119

Parkstone Grammar School, Poole

Lara Robinson (13) 120
Eliza Coyne (13) 122
Abi Fehrenbach (11) 124
Jessica Waring (16) 126
Jennifer Jenkins (12) 127
Ava Chapman (12) 128

Sharples School, Bolton

Bryan Beloti Lobo 129

St Andrew's RC Secondary School, Glasgow

John McGowan (16) 130
Alina Avelaoei (16) 132
Cara Mullen (17) 133
Maja Nowak (15) 134

Thomas Mills High School, Framlingham

Lilah Pinchin (11) 135
Emily Sheen (15) 136
Amelia Hawes (12) 138

Wexham School, Slough

Archie Clifford (14) 139
Alesha Samiullah (11) 140
Zara Ahmed (15) 143
Yusuf Saghir (11) 144
AbdulRafay Mohammed (16) 146
Tiana Bhattacharya (13) 148
Bida Kodakkadan (14) 150
Jane Joel (15) 152
Zainab Arsalan (11) 154
Erin Murphy (15) 155

Sahil Iqbal (12)	156
Christel Adjei (12)	157
Oliwier Krol (11)	158
Safiyah-Nur Mahmood (12)	159
Qaais Rashid (14)	160
Sanjay Chandran (13)	161
Jannat Mubashir (11)	162
Manha Fathima (14)	163
Franklina Adjei (11)	164
Maryam Moffatt (11)	165
Isaac Ifeanyi-Ukaeru (12)	166
Binyameen Alyas (12)	167
Sammar Fatima (13)	168
Aroona Aamer (11)	169
Natalie Muswati (15)	170
Shabbar Abbas (11)	171
Vishnu Divvela (13)	172

Wrotham School, Wrotham

Bertie Gregory (12)	173
Freya Hopkins (12)	174
Faridah Lawal (13)	176
Kian Pennell (12)	178
Maddie Santer (13)	179
Amelia Burtenshaw (12)	180
Zach Baker (13)	181

THE POEMS

BELIEVE!

FREEDOM

HONESTY

TRUTH

Dear Sky Brown

I've gone down in my own estimations
In relation to your teenage summer fame.
I've narrowly escaped actually listening to your interviews
By listening to the crowd in the background listening to you;
Sound is only so good a distraction.
You're a refraction of my insecurities.
Back in 2018, it was Malala.
I'd go as far as to say I've always had an idol to pray to,
Scrapbooked my own bible
From newspaper-clippings
Of women who listened to disillusioned masses
With a passion I've mastered after years of practice
But have no application for.
Sure, your dad's probably got industry connections
But you industriously connected the dots to success
Better than I ever coulda.
I shoulda just stayed in my room while you were sweating for the camera,
Helmet unclipped around your neck
like my dad never let me wear mine 'cause it was dangerous.
It's not like decades have passed;
If I'd been born somewhere else in the country
We coulda been singing
'Away In A Manger' together at primary.
Bet you've never cried for me like I've cried for you.

How many girls were left behind so you
Could smash bigger cracks in the glass ceiling
Than the ones they fell through?

Betsy Wragg (16)
Ballard School, New Milton

Our Lives, Not Yours

We are humans, not robots
We can make our own dreams and goals
We don't always need someone to tell us how to live our lives
Or their ways to change our future
We make our own futures
Our lives are like mountains, we climb so high only to get pushed down
It's like there is a boulder in front of us
We try to get past, but it's too big to push and it blocks the pathway up
But sometimes we want to get past, we need to get past, but we can't, so we give up
It's like feelings, we try to get past but it builds up so much that we just stop, we give up...
But always there is someone and something saying, "You can!" So you try
When it feels like it's too hard, just take a breath and then try some more and then...
The boulder is not there anymore
You can make your own dreams
Do not have anyone telling you that you can't, you can!

Evelyn Beatty (11)
Crickhowell High School, Crickhowell

I Can Perform

I am passionate about performing, acting, speaking aloud!
Singing, shouting - I could be so loud.
I can sing the highest notes and speak the loudest shout.
I can recite Shakespeare to a crowd in awe.

I can dance to melancholy songs with slow and steady
movements.
I can perform the greatest of plays of triumph,
Victory and defeat of lost lovers, only written in the stars,
Struck apart with every beat of their aching, beating hearts.

I can feel the emotions of a character on a page.
I can wear the pencil-drawn clothes
And feel the itchy fabric of the sketched-out suits.
I can bring them to life on a grand oak-carved stage
Or simply embody them for a few simple days.

I can breathe their feelings and hear their thoughts
But what is this talent, if I cannot perform?
The only chance I get to live as another,
To be as another is on a stage.
And I love the feeling of being another
And feeling as another
And I can only on stage.

If I cannot show them, to a crowd,
If I cannot be them, to a crowd they will be erased from my,
memory all thoughts aside.

I want to perform because I want to feel.
I want to be the character I saw in my mind.
I want to be able to feel their feelings
And live their life
Even if it's only for a short amount of time.

I cannot do that if I cannot perform.
When you play as Juliet or run with the feet of Aladdin,
The adrenaline of another's life
Of being in another's experience.

When you perform, you live another's life
And sing another song.
When you perform, you give life
To a being who only existed in a book,
Or who was only a name in a script,
A background character.

I want to perform because I want to feel.
I want to experience being another
Because it dazzles me and confuses me
How each individual is having a different, individual
Experience of life
And you will never be able to fully understand
Their individual experience of life.
And it angers me.

So I want to perform, so give me a chance.
To sing, to dance

To shout aloud, and cry
And live and love and act and perform.

So can I spread the message
About how just amazing it is
To live life through a character in a book?
From a song, from a story, to live as another?
Even if it's just for a few minutes?

Sophie Davenport (12)
Crickhowell High School, Crickhowell

Cold Calling

You know, cold calling can be really annoying sometimes,
You are focusing, and you have an answer,
But then your teacher makes you say it,
You think your classmates will judge you,
So you don't put your hand up,
But then the teacher decides you haven't talked enough yet,
so calls on you,
You have an answer, but you don't know what to say,
So you don't say anything, and your face starts turning red,
But you know what's worse?
When you were stretching, and it looks like you put your
hand up, but you didn't.
Maybe don't stretch in class.

It's probably good that this is all I'm worrying about,
However, it can be annoying when everyone's looking at you
and you don't know how to get them to stop,
I couldn't think of anything else to write about so...
I hope you liked the poem... that's all I wrote.

Katheryn Pratt (14)
Crickhowell High School, Crickhowell

Best Friends, Siblings, Parents, Spouses

Truth is underappreciated and overappreciated.
It can be tossed aside like rubbish in a bin or pleaded for like a beggar for food.
Truth can be a key freeing you from your prison or one hundred bricks being dumped on your shoulders,
It can fill your heart or break it.

"I love you."
The phrase everyone wants to hear.
The truth about someone's compassion for you.
The knowledge that someone cares about you: best friends, siblings, parents, spouses.

"I don't like you that much."
A sentence you only imagined in nightmares.
The truth that the person had given you hope only to have the door slammed in your face: best friends, siblings, parents, spouses.

"You're doing a great job."
The recognition you longed for, for trying your best.
The heart-warming feeling from the gratitude shown by someone you love: best friends, siblings, parents, spouses.

"No one deserves it more than her."
Being told that your hard work came to nothing and you don't deserve it.
The momentum you had built, diminished by a simple, seven words said to your face: best friends, siblings, parents, spouses.

"I missed you."
The confirmation that the feeling was mutual.
When you had to go away and were secretly dying inside from the distance,
They struggled too and are grateful to have you back: best friends, siblings, parents, spouses.

Silence.
The hard truth that someone is distancing themselves from you.
Years of building a bond, just to be broken by being cut off, nothing left to say to each other: best friends, siblings, parents, spouses.

Truth is so hard to distinguish nowadays. Knowing whether something is a rumour or a fact, the fear of being lied to or lied about.
Truth is needed for trust, to build relationships, and to unite us.
Truth, is it a burden or a gift?

Isabella Miles (16)
Crickhowell High School, Crickhowell

The Effect Of Our Doing

You, today, might look up and say, "What a wonderful world
we live in,"
That is a lie! A lie, I'm telling you!
So wipe your smile, yes wipe that grin,
For I have a poem for you to get through.

We say we have time, time to reverse our effects,
But I believe our time is over.
We're living in a loop, a loop of the world we bent,
You all must think you're jokers,
For our time is really over,
But you just won't listen!

It's all because we're young,
Greta will tell you a tonne,
And now I'm telling you a tonne,
Just like she, herself, would.

We're living in the after-effects,
The after-effects of our doings,
But it doesn't always have to be that way!

I today have words to say,
To stop your cheerful chirping.
This is not a game,
It won't be the same,
We will lose the world we live in.

So listen to us now,
For we are not too young,
We can change this world, I can show you how,
If you would just shut up and listen!

How we stop this is up to us,
For it is up to your actions,
If you keep our globe clean,
And my friend, I tell you, you'll see,
Soon our world could be just as you want to see.

Protect the oceans, protect the trees,
And we too can face the fears.

After these steps,
I'm telling you this,
Our world could be as beautiful as we wish to see,
Thank you,
Listener,
For your time.
I hope this touched you,
As much as it touches me.

Maddie Williams (13)
Crickhowell High School, Crickhowell

Who Are You?

Let me ask you something
To all the mixed race or black people out there
Do you know how it feels to be of mixed colour?
To belong to a different culture
To have different customs than your friends?
Let me ask you
Is it easy to know where you belong
Or where you want to belong?
It's not as easy as it seems
You think your life's planned out, but when you reach thirteen
That life completely changes
'Cause we all come in different ranges
And the people you know become strangers
Let me ask you
Are you sure you're not a stranger
Are you sure your parents know the true you
The good you
The bad you
The everything you
Are you even sure that you know who you are?
Are you white or are you black
Does that even define you?
Being mixed race isn't easy
Social media has got to our heads
When there are people out there, tanning their skin

Just to look like you
So why do you judge yourself
Why do think that you're not good enough?
Good enough for your friends
Good enough for your family
But most importantly are you good enough for yourself?
So, to all the mixed race or black people out there
Let me ask you
How does it feel?

Ann Thomas (12)
Crickhowell High School, Crickhowell

Lifeblood

Dead.
Yes, dead. That's the best way to describe it.
The keen blade of death has come
And it has left destruction in its wake.
Hillsides have been plastered into mosaics of green and brown,
Startlingly intensive monoculture has torn the lifeblood from the landscape.
Great beasts of steel and iron, sculpted from dark and indifferent hands,
Whirling and ripping apart the existence, flattening, crushing,
Corpses draped like cloth, stained with the blood of thousands.
Always the opposition holds the ace, you a two,
It reminds you of how insignificant of a being you are.
You can't,
You just can't, they say.
The voice of many drowning out the voice of the few.
The trees creak, the mighty oaks and the birches call,
avenge us, they say...
But,
Reality snaps back like elastic,
The many have gone, and all that remains is the voice of the few,
They say yes.
Yes?

Yes!
You can make a difference,
One person matters,
Do all you can and that is enough, more than enough
Speak out,
You have a voice for a reason,
All of life depends on you.
You may not be able to change the world,
But you can change their world.

Albie Hodgson (12)

Crickhowell High School, Crickhowell

Fitting In

We live in a world where the most important thing is fitting in,
To be like everyone else or to behave like them,
But what does it really mean?
When you determine yourself to be like everyone else,
And when everyone else is always copying each other to be 'cool',
But when you do end up fitting in
What happens then?
When you are popular
What is the point of all that work
Just to get the satisfaction of being cool?

But the big question is,
If we copy someone else to the point of it all,
It's just till someone stands out
Or says something to get the whole group of people's attention.
Or they do something cool
That satisfies them and everyone wants to be like them
And act like them?
And that's how the cycle begins,
Over and over again.

Making people think, *why aren't I like them?*
Or, *I wish I was them.*
But the real truth is that everyone is perfect

And no one needs to copy anyone else.
So just be yourself.
And also that's what being popular is all about,
Copying each other, but inside we all know it's all fake.

Imogen Johnson (11)
Crickhowell High School, Crickhowell

The Cost Of Peace

On a sunny summer day,
The sky falls grey.
An unknown is coming,
Something evil and cunning.
Fear spreads across a nation,
It's scared an entire population.

What is this thing that can bring people down to their knees?
And that can change the way of a summer breeze,

One word that's shaken an entire planet,
When you hear it you want to hide under a blanket.

War,
Conflict that has taken too many lives.
Only the luckiest has survived.

Throughout every country, there has been war,
Through every generation, there has been war,
Through everyone's blood, there is war.

Today it is still ongoing,
Why is it still growing?

The cries of the past still echo loud,
Yet leaders stand, defiant and proud.
Weapons raised, but what is won?
When homes are burned and hope is gone.

For every battle, there's a price,
A sacrifice of a human life.
But tell me, what will ever be enough,
When the cost of peace is paid in blood?

Tilly Sweetland (13)

Crickhowell High School, Crickhowell

The First Draft

Life's like the first draft,
You try and try then try again,
But nothing seems to work,
You decide to give up,
But there's that little voice inside you, that little glow,
It's saying "You might have 5 billion scrumpled-up pieces of paper,
But don't give up, you've got this, don't quit now,"
Then that little glow grows,
Then it gets bigger and *bigger* and *bigger!*
Until that once little glow grows,
And it spreads to your whole body,
You finally believe in yourself,
You picked yourself up,
You dusted yourself off,
You're glad you didn't give up,
You've done it,
Now you've got this amazing, beautiful human being,
Bet you're glad you didn't give up now,
Aren't you?

Lola-Rose Russell (12)
Crickhowell High School, Crickhowell

Our Perfect Day

Different people's 'perfect day' might be playing Fortnite,
Or staying up all night,
But mine is spending time with the people I love and care about,
Whether that be my friends or family.
They are the people I want to spend time with.

Some people might like going on adventures,
While others might like to stay at home,
Some like sleeping all day,
While others like going out and having fun.
I like doing both of those things,
Sometimes I like staying at home,
But sometimes I like going out and staying all day!

Well, whatever your perfect day is
No one can judge you because it is your perfect day and not theirs,
So just enjoy it because at the end of the day,
No one can really stop you!

Leila Elmore (11)
Crickhowell High School, Crickhowell

Shades

We walk the same world; we breathe the same air,
But some are judged by the shade we wear.
The colour of our skin, so rich and deep,
Should never decide the worth we keep.

Beneath we're the same, our hearts, our minds,
But racism is blind and makes people unkind.
Born of fear, hate, and ancient lies,
It divides the world before our eyes.

Why can't we see what's beyond the skin,
To the person, the spirit, the love they've grown.
For in every shade, there's joy and pain,
And dreams that shimmer like the sun through rain.

Let us shine above, break the chain,
See each other not for their skin.
For when we stand together, hand in hand,
The beauty of our differences will heal the land.

Haojin Zheng (12)
Crickhowell High School, Crickhowell

The Horror Of Depression And Suicide

Hundreds of thousands of people die each and every year
Dead by their own hands, stalked by depression before their deaths
Death is an unnerving but invertible thing that nothing can escape
In the end, they were in Depression's grip until their last breath filled the air

Depression is like a cloud of despair where death follows
Once depression has you in its jaws, is death all but assured?
Suicide rips apart friends and family
Leaving all in despair for this is not a subject to be taken lightly
For its next victim could strike close to home
Even you could be next
So, watch out and enjoy life to the fullest as that leaves you furthest from Death's door.

George Maglaras (12)
Crickhowell High School, Crickhowell

23

The Changing Year

In January when the trees are bare,
In February when there is frost in the air,
In March when the lambs don't seem to care,
In April when the flowers are suddenly there.

In May when the sun begins to shine,
In June when it's no longer dark at bedtime,
In July when the grapes swell on the vine,
In August when sunflowers climb.

In September when the leaves turn red,
In October when it's hard to get out of bed,
In November when fireworks explode above your head,
In December when Santa arrives on his sled.

Every month changes,
Every year the same,
A repeating pattern, an endless chain.

Cerys Tranter (13)
Crickhowell High School, Crickhowell

The Game Is Gone

The referee, so blind and so deaf,
It can't be long till the love for the game is gone.
The decisions, so poor and the timing so wrong,
It won't be long till the beautiful game is gone.

We have VAR and two linesmen,
Yet it feels like the ref couldn't care less.
A horror challenge is always ignored,
Yet kicking the ball away,
Is always seen and never ignored.

He ruins the natural flow of football,
He gives out cards like it's someone's birthday,
He's constantly near.
His decisions don't make any sense,
He is totally nuts,
And when the referee is near,
I am always in fear.

Tyler Whyatt (14)
Crickhowell High School, Crickhowell

Difference

"I'm fine," I say,
"No need for a call,"
"I don't think I can deal with this for much longer."
They kick me,
They punch me,
And throw me to the ground.

"Get up and walk it off," they say.
They cut me,
They threaten me,
They throw me to the ground,
"Get up and walk it off!" they chant.

Do they not realise,
How much I can take,
I might just go to a bridge,
And jump.
Don't they realise that they are just as different as me?

Many darker-toned people experience this too often.
Let's try to put a stop to this.

Gabriella Valentine (12)
Crickhowell High School, Crickhowell

The Blank Page

The blank page,
I'm stuck,
The page is not getting fuller,
The bright white is only getting getting whiter.
My head is searching and spinning becoming blanker than
the page,
Nothing,
Nothing is coming,
No ideas,
No hope of what to write.
Finally,
No, no, no,
And it's gone.
The blank page,
I'm stuck,
The page is not getting fuller,
The bright white is only getting getting whiter.
My head is searching and spinning becoming blanker than
the page,
Nothing,
Nothing is coming,
No ideas,
No hope of what to write.
Finally,
No, no, no,
And it's gone.

Rueben Kennah (13)

Crickhowell High School, Crickhowell

The Truth Of War

You hear the cries from children that used to be laughter,
Regular people trying to help,
Parents and children not knowing who's next or after,
Children and babies have dealt with this.

To see a shell-shocked baby isn't 'fine'!
Needing to flee a hospital that's going to be destroyed,
They think to themselves *why can't they be kind?*
All the rocks and rubble look like a void.

Digging family out of the rubble should not be a childhood memory,
To be hidden from the world, getting little to no help,
Just wanting to be treated fairly,
Wanting to be left to rest...

Yazi Habboub (13)
Crickhowell High School, Crickhowell

What To Do When You're Bored

When you're bored or all alone,
And you've not got anything productive to do,
Then listen to this poem.

When you're all alone and you just can't face it,
When you're on your own and you just can't brace it,
Maybe you could go outside,
Or stay inside and cry,
But hopefully, you're not a wimp,
So pause for now - come on and think.

You can play Minecraft, Roblox or Dirt Rally,
Among us, Mario, or Stardew Valley,
Or a board game like chess, Ludo,
Or Monopoly or Cluedo,
I mean, maybe you just need to download Pokémon Go
And get moving.

Sidney Miles (11)
Crickhowell High School, Crickhowell

Definition

Who am I?
My name does not matter.
What matters is how I define myself.
I am the books I enjoy reading.
I am karate.
Only you can define yourself.
Don't let others do it for you.
If people say you can't do something, don't listen to them.
Not everybody likes the same things.
It is horrific that we judge others based on their gender.
Their age.
People shouldn't assume that you like something just because other people do.
If they do that, don't be afraid to stand up and make your voice heard.
But that raises the question:
Who are you?

Lewin Thurston (11)
Crickhowell High School, Crickhowell

Poem

It doesn't matter what your skin tone is,
It doesn't matter if it's a hers or his.
We're all just people and that's what matters,
If you're big, if you're small, you'll understand when you hear it all.

Apples are green and strawberries are red,
But in the end they're both just fruits.
It doesn't matter if you're a substitute,
In football if you're black or white,
You're still playing the game even if you fight.

We all have soul and we all have an opinion,
It doesn't matter what it is.

Sam Taylor (12)
Crickhowell High School, Crickhowell

Who Am I?

Who am I?
Who am I? I don't know, I hope I'll find out as I grow
"What do you want to be?" people keep asking me over and over
My mind goes blank and I shrug my shoulders
I don't know what I want to be, I wish people would stop asking me
But I am something good I am something grand
It's gone better than I planned
I am brave
I've got friends that I've made
And a lovely family so really isn't that all that you need?
We're all different we're all united, so really, I'm very excited
For the future.

Georgia Gallop (11)
Crickhowell High School, Crickhowell

Hello But Goodbye

Hello, my worst enemy,
My biggest fear, and the one that taunts me.
Hello, I wish I could say goodbye, but
You will not let me. I wish I could take away the pain that you have caused me.
I wish I could help myself, but it feels like you're completely in control.
Hello, my worst nightmare, hello to you, food, the thing I should control,
But no, instead you control me.
But why am I like this? Why am I like many others cursed with you?
Why should I have to put up with you, the abuse that you bestow?
So to you, I say,
"Goodbye, my eating disorder."

Rylee Thomas (13)
Crickhowell High School, Crickhowell

Social Construct

Isolated, lost, detached from the rest of society,
All of these things cause propriety,
But it doesn't take much to see,
How it would be if you were not free.

Groups created amongst humanity, expressing hatred.
The discriminators and the discriminated.

The discriminators,
Never once want to dream,
What it would be to be on the other side, and scream.
Oh, loving hate.
They never set a date,
Of when they are planning to victimise.

The discriminated,
Always hope,
How they will learn to cope.

Oliwia Rajner (14)
Crickhowell High School, Crickhowell

"We Didn't Grow Up Like This," They Say

Our world, our home, is getting destroyed,
Not just by pollution, but by technology, deployed.
We do not look up, we just look down,
Other generations wear a frown.
We didn't grow up like this," they say,
We didn't want it to be this way.
Soon, people might as well not exist,
With AI growing and growing, I insist!
Now is our time to act,
Before the massive impact.
Do you want humans to thrive?
Come on, let us take a dive.
We can fix this, you know we can,
Come on, everybody, let us make a plan!

Sophia Jones-Griffiths (12)
Crickhowell High School, Crickhowell

We Are Like Fruits

Good days are like good fruits,
Some last three days, sometimes three months,
But bad fruits last long,
Like tinned fruits, the durian fruit and so on,
But we can change that,
Because fruits are like people, we're all different,
Good and bad, it is not about the look but the taste,
No fruit is the same, no human is the same,
We might be in a group or culture, but no fruit is the same,
Let this be a reminder we cannot change the past,
But we can change the future,
We are different, keep the good, change the bad.

Cain Denney (11)
Crickhowell High School, Crickhowell

The Earth's Demise

From the depth of the ocean
Things are always in motion
We used up the planet
Everything's gone so can it

Polar ice is melting
Soon it'll be a has-been
Forests are on fire
The planets about to expire

The planet's an oven
It's now or it's nothing
We were supposed to be utopian
But now we are dystopian

The planet's about to die
You never know 'til you try
There isn't time to just sit
There's still time to save it.

Elis Jones (13)
Crickhowell High School, Crickhowell

37

The Greatest Sport

Football is a sport
With fans for support
It doesn't matter what race
Or the colour of your face

In the stands, you hear the crowd
Screaming and chanting very loud
They fill you with pride
As you play against the opposition side

As you score that goal
Or you're fouled to the ground
Or you get subbed off
The feelings flow around

If you ever miss a shot
Your teammates will console you
Or if your shot gets caught
Your teammates are there for you.

Lewis Schofield (11)
Crickhowell High School, Crickhowell

The Story Of A Truth

A truth yearning, a silent sin,
Buried in shadows, it longs to shine,
To break free, to make things right.

A heavy burden, a crushing weight,
A truth untold, a tragic end.
But when it's revealed, a change takes place,
A healing balm, a fresh new space.

The doubts and fears that once held away,
Are now scattered like stars in an obsidian sky.
For in its freedom the truth finds its voice,
It will reveal secrets, and in its finality, it finds its peace.

Lyra Kaur (12)
Crickhowell High School, Crickhowell

The Blackbird

One spring morning,
The robins were singing,
And the fridge was humming,
All was at peace, or was it?
The blackbird was in the darkest tree,
In the coldest corner,
Longing for a way out,
The bird was trapped, swallowed by its feelings,
The robins sang their songs of harmony,
But the blackbird had a mission,
He was going to be seen,
He was going to make it,
He was strong,
He was powerful,
That was all he needed,
But he couldn't see it.

Jenson Jones (13)
Crickhowell High School, Crickhowell

An Artist's Canvas

Art is subjective,
It doesn't matter what adjective you put before it,
But everyone's art is still different,
It's like a canvas has feelings,
Sometimes they give the impression that they are sad,
Like the artist has been having a bad day,
The swirls and the patterns,
The paint and the pencils,
The use of the shade and texture,
All come together to make something truly wonderful,
Just like a human.

Daphne Smith (11)
Crickhowell High School, Crickhowell

Italy

Italy,
Pasta, pizza, gelato, tiramisù
Italy, the best place for food.
Pasta, pizza, gelato, Tiramisù
Spiedini in the barbecues
Italy has so many beautiful views
Pasta, pizza, gelato, tiramisù
The Mona Lisa was stolen from France
With the Italian's dance
You take a glance
And do not want to leave
Italy
Pasta, pizza, gelato, tiramisù
Italy is the place for you.

Emma Neill (12)
Crickhowell High School, Crickhowell

Are There Still Beautiful Things?

The promises we made to keep this world clean,
Was this all misleading?
The sun shines and the birds sing,
But in the end, we all go to sleep.
Forests burn and disasters happen,
If we refuse to address these problems,
What would the world be like now?
Plants aren't thriving and animals are dying,
People are starving and wars are coming.
The question is,
Are there still beautiful things?

Isobel Rumsey (13)
Crickhowell High School, Crickhowell

Rugby Community

Bringing people together
Everyone on the team's a brother
Past teams lurk like phantoms
Choirs bellowing anthems

Fifteen men prepared for war
Fans waiting for more
The size of them is quite a sight
Oppositions hide in the night

Oval balls flying round the pitch
Teams battered and left in a ditch
Extraordinary strength from all around
Wails from fans around the ground.

William Creed-King (14)
Crickhowell High School, Crickhowell

Happiness Is Contagious

Happiness is contagious
It's like a flu
When I smiled at someone
They smiled too
Now imagine if happiness was lost
Imagine how much that would cost
Without happiness, we would all be doomed
This would be a deep wound
Thinking about being happy
I realised its worth
A smile like mine could orbit the Earth
Keep smiling keep the skill perfected
Keep the world infected.

Diksha Subedi (14)
Crickhowell High School, Crickhowell

Everyone's Different

I call myself, well, it does not matter what my name is.
Skin tone does not matter because everyone is different.
With opinions, they're all cool like religion, it is just a belief.
Does not mean you must believe it, yes.
Personally, I like football and cricket.
They are out of this world.
They are so amazing and so crazy but it does not matter if you do not
Like them, yeah, yeah, ooh yeah!

Mohammad Bojang (11)

Crickhowell High School, Crickhowell

Be You

Be you
We are people, not robots, or anything you want to treat us
like
We can create our own dreams, goals, and futures
We can be anything if we put our minds to it and work hard
for it
Do not change to fit in, just love you for you
The world changes and so will you. Do not think it's such a
terrible thing
We are all different shapes and sizes - we are never the
same
Just be yourself.

Ariana Thomas (11)

Crickhowell High School, Crickhowell

Children Of The Earth

Across the world,
In another land,
Children of happiness,
Play in the sand,
These children know happiness,
But they also know sadness,
Emptiness, loneliness,
These children, far away,
Not our concern,
Why should we care...?
Because that could have been us,
You and me,
Living in anger and pain,
Knowing every day that was our destiny,
Our purpose.

Teddie Trainer (13)
Crickhowell High School, Crickhowell

Sheep In The Tractor

Rural farm terror!
There are sheep in the tractor!
Go run for your life!

Cows are on it too.
With a combine harvester.
Humans beware!

They fought for an age.
Mortal combat with tractors.
Why'd I write this?

If you find a metaphor in here you are truly mad.
This is meant to be a humorous romp and has no hidden
meaning whatsoever.

Felix Turner (12)

Crickhowell High School, Crickhowell

The Hidden Truth

As the darkness emerges, the sun does rise,
The world full of lies, the truth does fly,
With one wrong move, we might lose,
But the truth will always lie, across the borderline.

The hidden truth, meaningfully despised,
The truth is beautiful, plentiful for some,
If we hide within lies, it floods the prize,
The truth is beautiful, so why do we hide?

Bethany Button (14)
Crickhowell High School, Crickhowell

You're Just Stuck...

Imagine your life as you're standing in a queue,
It goes on and on, and feels as if it would never end,
It goes nowhere, and neither do you.

But then you see your destination,
It's like a glint of hope,
You feel like you can do it.

Once you try and try,
After the blood, sweat and tears,
You see you're finally there.

Tilly Phillips (14)
Crickhowell High School, Crickhowell

The Dragon's Heart

He is the heart of our nation
The one that carried us all
Through times of darkness
He showed us light.
He is Gareth Bale.
He is the Dragon's Heart.

His feats are unbelievable
Five Champions Leagues at Madrid.
Making Wales unstoppable
He is the Welsh GOAT.
He is Gareth Bale.
He is the Dragon's Heart.

George O'Farrell (14)

Crickhowell High School, Crickhowell

Change In Football

In football,
there's change.
For example, the Premier League,
when teams go up and down,
and there's a new winner and a new loser every year.
Change is key.
Also, players can change;
you have one player and
the next thing you know
their son or daughter is playing,
so change is real
and is how football works.

Joseph Cleaves (11)
Crickhowell High School, Crickhowell

The Beautiful Game

It is the passion to support the players on the pitch,
The adrenaline of the game,
The uproar and murmur of the crowd,
It encapsulates you, heart drumming in your chest.
It is the loyalty, identity, and inclusivity to be a part of
something much bigger than yourself.
The thunderous chants washing around the stands,
electrifying the atmosphere.

Cerys Griffiths (13)
Crickhowell High School, Crickhowell

There Is No Planet B

There is no Planet B, you must see.
Don't be mean, keep it green.
At the end of the day, no matter what we say,
Plant a tree, set the Earth free.
If you cannot reuse, refuse.
Go green, breathe clean.
Let's work as a team, the easier it will seem.
And tackle through climate change!

Nicole Wilton (14)
Crickhowell High School, Crickhowell

In The Shadow Of The Bomb

As It lowers, rain falls.
Sirens below, screams are heard.
An orange glow fades to black.
Buildings fall, people collapse.
Flames ignite, smoke rises.
The news shows, families mourn.
Sirens fade, screams are deafened.
The city is no more.

George Dunkling (12)
Crickhowell High School, Crickhowell

A Good Day

A good day is when you get to sit next to your friends on the
bus
Or when you get positive points.
When you have a good day,
You might have gone to the park with your friends,
Or when you see waffles at lunch.
Now that is what I call a good day.

Myles Rumsey (11)
Crickhowell High School, Crickhowell

The World Of Rugby

Rugby
Year by year new teams come to play
Year by year new players play
Year by year new players become champions
Year by year another team lifts the trophy
Year by year teams go up leagues
Year by year teams move down a league.

Liam Davis (11)
Crickhowell High School, Crickhowell

School

I'm caged in school,
Trapped! Nowhere to move,
I feel like I'm too cool,
I just really disapprove.

I'm tired,
I'm drained,
Let me free,
I can't explain my desire to be entertained.

Rhian Williams (14)

Crickhowell High School, Crickhowell

Beach

Waves crashing onto the sand, grabbing it, so they do not
slip away
People screaming as they jump over the waves
Shells scattered everywhere like sprinkles on a cake
The salty smell of the beach filled the air.

Elsie Callender (11)
Crickhowell High School, Crickhowell

Sports

Sports is a thing everyone loves,
no one hates it.
I love sports,
you love sports,
we all love sports.
If you lose or if you win,
it does not matter,
we enjoy it.

Goutham Valanath (11)

Crickhowell High School, Crickhowell

The Beautiful Truth

Can beauty truly be described via our means of word?
A concept foreign, yet comforting by all means,
Beauty in bird song,
Or a forest near, untouched, pristine?

Or is beauty more a word we give a meaning,
Because we can't fully grasp the reality?
We can't see what makes something beautiful,
So we try to undermine and belittle its greatness.
Maybe beauty is a way of expressing our anger at
something,
The acknowledgement that we are now inferior to some
other.
Is that what makes something beautiful?

Or is beauty more a measure of our admiration,
Of something we see as innately pleasing to our eyes?
Our own sense of entitled definition defines a beautiful
thing,
Not necessarily the truth, yet a fact worldwide.

Some animals we call ugly,
We frown on a concept we ourselves created.
But why?
Because maybe beauty doesn't mean anything at all,
Rather, not mean anything in the grand scheme.
Because a Supernova doesn't intend to be pretty,
Radiant,

So beautifully stunning, that men would fight to just catch a
glimpse.
It doesn't think of itself,
Because it has no thought,
But still arranged by order in a moment of infinite chaos,
It demonstrates something perhaps we don't get.
To know of a thing is one thing,
To understand it is another.
But to admire something,
That perhaps may be the purest thing of all.

When we unshackle our notion of humanity and look upon
our world with wonder,
Do we see it any differently?
Does an idea change the way the stars look?
Does a thought make the hummingbird's colour become
anything other than mesmerising?
Maybe beauty isn't ours to decide after all.
Because we barely know real beauty ourselves,
From our treatment of the Earth,
Is our desecration of nature our gift to a beautiful thing?

Maybe we should change the definition of beauty,
Because something not truly beautiful can't fully grasp a
concept of true beauty.
Human evil isn't beautiful,
Yet humanity is.
Beauty and ugliness don't fight over which should be
dominant,

Because there is no real way of saying which is better.
Perhaps beauty comes from uniformity?
Perhaps there is no true beauty, apart from the absence of ugliness.
Ugliness in appearance no, but instead of character and meaning.
A supernova heralds about a new beginning perhaps,
But at the cost of something else.

Beauty cannot exist without a sense of ugliness,
Because then nothing would be beautiful, nor could it be ugly.
Without one, the other shouldn't exist,
Because then how could we possibly know of one without the other?
Maybe we as a society,
A community of individuals,
Should stop calling things beautiful because we decide they are.
We aren't a pure people, for we hate and hurt.
Maybe beauty doesn't truly exist,
Maybe beauty is what makes up everything.
All I know is that we don't deserve to define what that really means.
A concept foreign, yet familiar.
Known, but not understood.
Beauty is a word, I think we can all agree.
But what should that word mean?

Should it highlight an idea that may not exist?
For a person doesn't naturally grow to enhance their
beauty.
Beauty isn't a natural thing perhaps then,
But then what is it?
Maybe it's nothing,
And by now it's too late to change it.

We'll have to live with a mistake then,
I suppose.

Freddie Lockett (14)

Dartford Grammar School, Dartford

Poem

You talk about karma
Yet we are 'uneducated'
You tantalise your tastebuds
With our food you call 'dirty'
I am Indian
So it's fine to do that?

I am told I am 'burnt'
'Burnt' and different
You mock our accents
Yet exoticize others

Assumptions make our hearts transparent
My personality is lifeless from the mistreatment
Caged in echoes of your words

Swept away and told to deal with it
Treated like something trivial
The unwanted attention the heartless give me
Turns my mind into a storm of questions
Why me?
But wait, I'm Indian
So it's fine to do that?

End racism, you said
As you called my culture 'odd'
My eyes no longer see you as a person

But as the being who made my mind pessimistic
Pessimistic knowing what you'd do each day

You trap me in a cell
Forcing me to endure your hate and evil
You have deactivated all joy in my heart and turned it into
fear
Shunning me and stealing my self-worth

Your words of sheer malevolence
Are simply
Wrong..

But I am Indian.
So it's fine to do that?

But one day the beautiful truth will arrive
The one that will end your ignorance
And teach you reality.

Paramveer Chodha (14)

Dartford Grammar School, Dartford

Honeycomb

Here is my piece of art: my honeycomb
Born from the lamenting pollen
Scattered and buried on the battlefield
By you.

After you believed unconditional sweetness was deserved
If with your delicate hands
You planted some flowers.

Romantically your eyes hum to the sound of Dirge,
Tears drop one by one with calculation.
Then the sun dims: its eyes, the celestial blinks
Null clouds run over the hollow,
Avant-garde conformists - you reveal to my hive

The contrast of your soul; and the gold you declare,
Painted your masterpiece.

Not prismatic or innocent,
My honeycomb, born from scorn
Is bleeding. Like a healthy

Furious heart quietly
Pressing out the burnt salts of war.
Red rose and satin heart you say?

My passion is misinterpreted.
Proud eyes decorated by flowers
Fail to glimpse through the petals

To see the bees in puddles of their own
Sweet, sweet honey.
Discarded winged coins you didn't bother to pick up.

Now I invite you to grasp my artwork in your hands -
Take a bite out of this honeycomb,
Let your teeth tremble from its sweetness,

Smell the sugar and apathy falling from the night.
Their repose silent; I can only respect
As their artisan.

Hieu Tran (15)
Dartford Grammar School, Dartford

If Only I Had A Chance

I have heard the sigh of those in yearning and sorrow,
Sweeter than a pot of honey,
In the pursuit of full truth, I have been dissolved in universal fraud,
To achieve the beautiful truth is nothing but a spherical ball of lies,
The fiery orb which settles in the westerly horizon is sewn by the needles of lies and misfortune,
The park, which sought grass and water, is mantled of what I cannot see,
It seeps into every nook and corner,
I fret to gaze over the snowy peak, only for the truth to be concealed by a huddle of gaping tourists,
I go on an evening saunter in the spirit of what can be discovered in this world of fruit and tale,
And is quickly shunned by yearning and longing,
A lie can bask in the shade of today and cripple in the scorch of tomorrow,
But, what about the centuries to come?
They will thirst for a past and smirk at the thought of what is left, of what is,
I can't do what he does, I can't start and complete what many have left us to complete,
The beautiful truth is reliant on the service of those who don't wear the suit,

Of those who are on the front and fuel the nation at its lowest,
The ones that tie the rope between today and tomorrow.

Shaunak Shinde (14)
Dartford Grammar School, Dartford

Am I Alone?

Why does it feel like I'm not respected?
Why does it feel like I haven't grown?
Why does this feeling leave me dejected?
Why does it feel like I'm alone?

I'll dance between the fake reality
Looking to a place called home
But is it really what it feels like?
Or is it a prison-like dome?

Show me a mirror that'll reflect the real me
Something that the world can accept
Am I blind? I cannot see
Lost in the sea of tears I wept

Can you make this home feel like freedom
If I tell you who I am?
Can you see the person within me?
Am I just a scam?

My world, made up of lies
Has one shining truth
A truth I'm not fond of
A truth I hide from in sin

Maybe I like to have a breakdown
Maybe I'm just insecure

Maybe I don't know who I'm friends with
Maybe I'm just not sure.

Austin Joby (14)
Dartford Grammar School, Dartford

Childhood Time Travellers

I rested on the wooden bench in the rain,
In my green leggings, and blue T-shirt,
Because I hated dresses,
I despised the intricate frills and the itching patterns,
And the fact that only princesses wore them,
I knew I was no princess
And so wearing my pink dresses was always disappointing,
No matter what I hoped I'd look like.

And I hid behind the pine tree,
Whilst the other kids laughed and played
And I wondered how tall I could climb,
If I had someone to climb with,
The branches were broad and rich maroon,
Secure and safe to rest on,
But would that be the case if I was conscious of the invisible
friend next to me?

And my eyes stung when they named me dumb for my hair,
So I wept in the bathroom,
And snipped at the golden edges,
Until I couldn't cut anymore, my fingers bloody, my eyes
puffy,
I loved to read and learn, to run and to play,
But when I looked in the mirror, I wanted to hate being
smart.

I was told that I was loved,
But never did I let myself believe such things,
If I can't love myself, neither can you,
You aren't allowed to,
Your love is suspicious because I don't deserve it.

I knew a girl back then,
And once I knew her cheeky, hazel eyes,
I search for them every day,
But I find them in no one,
For the truth is,
You can always return to the past, but there is nobody there
anymore.

So I beg you, time travellers,
Find the blonde, fun-loving, hazel-eyed six-year-old,
And wrap your arms around her one last time,

Before she grows up.

Eloise Key
Exeter School, Exeter

Swimming Lessons

When I was three, I had swimming lessons
Puffy arm bands keeping me afloat
My podgy hands splashing pointlessly
Afraid but safe in my parents' hands.

When I was six, I had swimming lessons
Circling around and around the pool
Clinging to the wall if I panicked
Skill-less but happy.

When I was eight, I had swimming lessons
Slowly separating from the wall
Widths across the pool
Each one harder but only a little way from safety.

When I was ten, I had swimming lessons
Going to my first competitions
Parents watching judgingly
The pressure building slowly.

Now I am twelve, and I have swimming lessons
Go faster
Breathe less
But I'm inhaling water
I want to go back.

Leia Beckmann (13)
Exeter School, Exeter

Friendship

As laughter filled the air,
Joy filled me,
The rain raged outside,
Yet I'm here with no care for the outside,
All I needed lay here,
Before my very own eyes,
All night was a peaceful battle,
Hurricanes seethed, though I had what I needed,
The most beautiful, noxious storm came with the
Most captivating truth.

This wasn't over when the
Weather shuffled to a misty morning,
Nor will it change as we grow older,
Or when they find home in other directions,
This will never change,
Because this is friendship.

Harriet MacGregor

Exeter School, Exeter

The Class Clown

Walk in
Crack a smile
Make a joke

They laugh
Of course they do
Because it's you
The class clown

Inside, it hurts
Outside, hollow joy
Alone
The laughter is deafening
Together
We are strong

Those who understand
Your pain
Your fellow clowns
They understand
The feeling of the crack inside
The emptiness in your laughter
Alone

You are the class clown.

Belle Goulden (12)
Exeter School, Exeter

The Sun

I know it hurts, trust me I do, but one day the sun will shine through.
When the darkest thoughts seep into your mind, and if love and friendship should turn blind.
I'm hurting so bad, and I can't tell anyone what I truly feel.
How uncomfortable I feel nearly every second I keep this bottled in.
And then I remember... it's going to be okay.
I know it hurts, trust me I do, but now the sun has shone through.

Everleigh Laing (12)
Exeter School, Exeter

Made Up

We each have our own truth.
Our own identity,
Our own fears,
Our own personalities,
Which all make up who we are as individuals.

We are made up of dreams,
Of hopes, of futures, of nightmares -
Which haunt us in sleep
And taunt us in wakefulness.

We are made up of memories,
The lives we have lived and the tales we have told.
Our brain, which clings onto whispers of names and faces
Recycles the moments that make us human
And creates images for us to remember them by.

We are made up of each other,
The people we surround ourselves with -
Our friends, our family,
People who make us the best version of ourselves we can
be.

We are made up of those who came before us,
Our ancestors, our family tree
Which branches through history

And takes root in stories and legends -
Passed down through generations
Ending with you or me.

Lisa Jarrett

Haywards Heath College, Haywards Heath

Aspirations In Despair

Isolated and alone,
The only company is my phone.
Captured in-between four walls,
Agreeably society is at fault.
The youth glued to screens,
Blue light LED beams.
Hiding away our personalities,
Being prisoners to technology,
Our elders need a heartfelt apology.
As we are captive, free me!

This cycle must be broken,
I feel as if I have been internally woken.
Yearning to be a part of another generation,
Perchance by then, it will be a completed operation,
My only optimism is my dreams,
Which are confined in my schemes.
As soon, the world will be my oyster,
An opportunity to be roister.
Hibiscus flowers embedded in my hair,
Beaches and mocktails I'll be aware.
Volcanos, mountains and landscapes,
Will be clasped in my palm after I escape.
Finally, I'll be free,
Seeing capitals: Vienna, Paris and Tenerife.

Annie Ghag
Haywards Heath College, Haywards Heath

Tearful War

I survived that war
But it will always haunt me in my mind
How happy I was before
And how I had to go out of my home
That created my own folklore
All of my friends that I have lost
And all of that love that I don't have any more
I waited for an explanation
But your plan was to ignore
I shed my tears and blood
Which was what I unhoped for
The jokes weren't funny
And this is the truth I will always speak for
Because no one will ever know how hard it was
To stand on that floor
And smile every day
Giving all of my sweat for
Nothing that matters to me
This is the truth I stand for
And this is how I really feel
Because I started to adore
My words, my accent, my ethnicity and myself
And this is what I'm proud for
I will miss my old life
And I know I will forevermore
But I'm so grateful now

That I survived
Even if I will be always fighting
In that tearful war.

Nelly Pandey

Haywards Heath College, Haywards Heath

The Unseen Truth

Every mean comment to the next,
All of the false rumours being spread around,
Sometimes I wish all of this would end,
We have insecurities that don't make us feel proud,

Maybe we want to go missing,
Disappear for a while,
All of the mean messages spamming our phones; *ping, ping, ping*
We can hide anything under a smile,

This world isn't perfect,
Overprotective parents; no parents,
People get treated with tonnes of disrespect,
Sometimes people don't know what it's like to be loved,

Always being left out,
That always makes us feel that we aren't good enough,
Do people realise that some people are struggling? I doubt it,
We can still act 'happy' even though some times are rough,

It only takes one mean word to hurt someone,
Making them feel that they are the main problem,
Blaming themselves for something they didn't do,
This could mean the end for some.

Lillie-Mae Gill (14)
Honley High School, Honley

Ideals

Social media is feeding you all the lies
that keep on eating you up inside
and when you cry under your bedsheets late at night
look in the mirror, asking,
Why can't I disappear?
and, why can't it just be clear,
that girls on your screens are not what they seem;
with their small waists and their pretty faces,
flashing bright lights in your face, saying,
"Buy this, buy that, and you too can look like me"?
Okay, on the outside they may have all the ideals,
but on the inside how do they feel,
counting every calorie of every meal,
painting their face every day to meet the ideals
of a place we once called home but is now a battlefield?
Social media is not what it seems,
the girls on your screens
go to sleep every night
bundled up tight,
in a guilt of their own creation.

Jess Gledhill (14)
Honley High School, Honley

Dare To Deny

Truth is a beauty in itself,
Undeniable,
Pure,
Reliable.
On it, cities were built, a solid foundation,
But lies yield ruin only.
Always watching,
Like a hawk or caring parent,
You choose.
Some see it as a ruler to measure,
Others a hindrance to their pleasure.
However, the truth remains steadfast,
Anchor unmoving in the storm.
Objective, not subjective,
It stood the test of time,
Rome fell, independence gained, countries formed.
But the truth remains unchanged.
Society can be demanding,
But the truth is still withstanding.
In a world filled with darkness, unrest and deceit.
A light shone.
Accept it, reject it, hide?
That light is my truth.
Is it yours?

Isabella-Rose Dent (13)

Honley High School, Honley

Brother, Forever

My brother from the start
We are more than blood
He's a part of my heart
No one ever understood

He's the light in the dark
I'm the sea, he's the ark
I'm sure he has other heroes
But he is mine for a lifetime

When he went out the door and left
It broke my heart
But you had to start your quest
After all, it's for the best

Even though the hallways are hollow
From your protecting soul
The footsteps you make, I'll follow
I'm now alone with one goal

You'll forever be my brother
And not because we share the same father or mother.

Aniela Szewczyk (13)
Honley High School, Honley

Waiting In The Room Between

I'm cold.
They've given me an ugly grey jumper to wear over my hospital gown,
the plasticky fabric dress only reaching my mid-thighs.
It doesn't really help.
Cold.
The walls of the waiting room are all white,
cheaply-framed children's drawings adorning too much blank space.
Cold.
The bare skin of my legs has broken out in goosebumps,
shaking against the creaky plastic chair they've sat me in.
Cold.
Maybe I just can't feel warmth anymore.

A clipboard sits on my lap, a neatly printed questionnaire.
I feel anything but neat.
Raw.
I'm just a dog in a kennel now,
a declawed, matted girl
whose bite has never done enough damage anyway.
Raw.
I'm nervously clicking the pen they've given me,
the space between the sounds just long enough to hurt.
Raw.
I feel split in half, waiting like this;

ripped into two versions of myself,
both with bleeding, jagged edges.

I'm in that headspace they like me in,
the kind they always drag me to by my bloody, bruised
throat.
Pliable.
I should've known what they were doing,
leaving me alone like this.
Pliable.
Just another way to torture me.
To put on a puppet show where I'm the lead,
sobbing on all fours in the spotlight.
Pliable.
I want to scream at the injustice,
at the weight of all they've done to me.
I swallow those words instead.
Maybe somewhere deep in my belly,
they'll take root and grow.

The nurse stands over me, and I tell her I'm sad.
I'm so sad.
Pain.
Small, simple words, the only ones that make sense
as I clutch at my chest like a child
and point to where it hurts.
Pain.
I realise then that I'm crying.

It isn't normal, the way I do this,
just tears showing up on my cheeks.
I'm not even sure they're coming from my eyes;
it feels more like being wrung out, like a sponge.
Pain.
I've felt terror like this before -
it's familiar, but still horrible and electrifying,
whipping up a frenzy of needles inside my chest.

My head flops forward a bit,
and the nurse gently manoeuvres it back up.
Close.
Her palm cups my cheek for just a second,
and I think I might cry at the gentleness of it all.
Close.
It's terrifyingly vulnerable,
being subjected to her care like this,
and I can't help but feel like a hummingbird being held in a
bear's paws.
Close.
I push her away, almost cringing at the bluntness of it.
But I know it needs to be harsh
because that's how it feels inside me.

The sunset streams through the windows -
objectively beautiful,
flickering warmth on the chair to my right.
Waning.

It hits me, but I'm not comforted.
It only makes my shadow so much bigger,
a bruise that follows wherever I go.
Waning.
I feel like a shucked oyster,
pried apart and exposed;
like someone's used a crowbar to crack open my ribs,
leaving my beating heart out in the open for everyone to
poke at.
Waning.
My hair is wet.
I vaguely remember taking a bath,
trying to scrub all the grime off myself.
Even if it's gone,
I can still feel it clinging to my nerves.

The dirt has sunk into my pores;
I will never be able to get it out.
I feel the absence of the kind nurse acutely,
my chest aches with the ancient weariness,
and the waiting room remains cold.

Grace Jones-Parker (17)
HSDC, Havant

Purple Butterflies

I wake up with fear in my heart,
Another Monday morning, I don't want to start,
Dreading, overthinking, did I start this war?
With my green olive jumper, my stomach makes a roar!
It feels like purple fluttering butterflies stirring inside,
I hop on the bus for an anxious ride,
Another day just starting, another day of pain,
Will they talk to me, will they shove me, will they push me away?
Will they call me names or will they not,
Dread and thoughts stirring like a pot,
Then it happened, the worst thing of all,
They hit me, they shoved me, they pushed me into a wall,
When I walked past they gave me a scary look!
I stood there startled and shook,
All of the children saw me running past,
I ran to the bus out of breath and fast,
Wiping my teary eyes, why are they so cruel,
As I sit on the bus, get me out of this school,
While I wrap my arms around my mother, I say,
Please, not tomorrow, not another day!

Erin Osmond (12)
Llangatwg Community School, Cadoxton

Truth

Age three: she's going to be heartbroken.
Age nine: she's going to have to run away from the boys.
Age fifteen: her dress is way too short.
Age seventeen: do you crave male attention?
When will it stop? Never good enough, never attractive enough,
Too attractive, nerdy, stupid, too skinny, too fat, either ignored or left alone.
"Boys will be boys."
"That's what men do."
The most narcissistic, self-centred, hurtful mindset ever.
They wear what they want with no care in the world.
No judgement, no comments.
The guilt of just existing as a woman in this generation.
It's too much.
"Women are this,"
"Women are that,"
"That woman is too thin,"
"That woman is too fat."
Women are human.
Treat them like it.
It's not all men, but women suffer.
As women lie dead awake, thinking to themselves:
Am I a mistake?
An object, a project?
I just want to get along.

Man or bear?

If I were attacked by a bear, they wouldn't say, "Well, what did you wear?"

Kali Davies (12)

Llangatwg Community School, Cadoxton

War Is All To Them

War?
A war is configured on both sides
They forget who receives the low blow
Those who stayed to feel sanctuary
Are made to decide the fight
Casualties are created from the uncaring heart
Deaths are imminent from those who are unwelcome
War is waged on the innocent
War creates a mist of crimson blood
War creates casualties
Casualties create disasters
Disasters are massacres
Massacres are war
Communities end in war
War ends communities
War is the problem
War is for land
War is for pride
War creates deaths
War divides those who love
War kills those who hate
We must kill the war
Instead of killing those whom you love
Help those who you love to kill the war
War is a problem
The problem is the war

The problem with humankind
Is those who fight in the war.

Alexander Rowland (14)
Llangatwg Community School, Cadoxton

McDonald's

Walk into McDonald's, let's see what they sell,
Must be something delicious, because I can smell,
The way the burger sizzles,
Tasty chocolate drizzles,
The super salty chips,
With every ketchup dip,
The sweet apple pie,
The way time makes me cry,
But the chicken nuggets are great,
When munching with your mate,
The ice cream is a dream,
But broken machines make me scream!
The crisp, the smell, the taste,
Chicken tenders never go to waste,
A Big Mac will make you drool,
Ordering fillet o' fish, you're a fool,
The best place is McDonald's,
With best friends like Ronald,
When they're closed, it makes me sad,
Because I want McDonald's so bad,
But it's okay,
I'll see Ronald on a different day.

Savannah Davies (12)
Llangatwg Community School, Cadoxton

Who Am I?

I am enough,
I am me, and me is I,
Who is me? I also ask,
Sometimes my life feels like a heavy task,
Sometimes I've had enough at the end of the day,
Sometimes I feel like I don't have a say,
Sometimes I feel happy too,
Other times all I want to say is boohoo,
But even if my day was rough,
I always know, I am enough,
So, who is me?
Well, even though I might not be everyone's cup of tea,
I am proud of myself because I am me,
If you need to comment on me, maybe look at yourself,
I know I have a perfect life,
And that when I grow up, I'll be more than 'his' wife,
But even if the day was tough,
I always know, I am enough.

Jasmine Evans (14)
Llangatwg Community School, Cadoxton

Perfection?

Perfect pictures with a thousand filters,
Perfect models with a hundred fillers.

You can't be fat, you have to be size ten.
Do I need to be a Barbie to match my Ken?
My worth isn't measured by a scale.
I shouldn't be judged, female or male.

We are judged every second, on and off the screen.
This generation's mental health is the worst we've ever seen.
My body isn't the problem - it's the people who judge it.
We might not be slim, but we are still fit.

Our bodies are right,
So stop telling us how to shape them.
Lumps, bumps, stretch marks, curves:
It's all these things that make us unique.

Lily Crumb (12)

Llangatwg Community School, Cadoxton

Remember To Recycle

Behind the rocks where all the creatures lay at the end of
the day,
Where the lumpy smooth slimy creatures go to rest after a
long day away,
Every little grain of sand to the smallest fish swimming in
the sea,
No matter what we have to keep it clean.
All the pollution that is happening is unacceptable.
The beach is a home for animals just like how a roof over
our head that we call a home,
Imagine your house being destroyed.
Cute little creatures are crying, at the minute,
They are traumatised by having no home to go to.
Here at the beach the creatures need help and good citizens
like you
Can help by stopping littering and remember to recycle.

Evie Hawkes (11)

Llangatwg Community School, Cadoxton

I Am

I am the friend who had feelings pushed on
I am the person who can't go out
I am the one that some people find weird
I am stuck with my own thoughts
I am always there for people
I am full
I am a farmer
I am a swimmer
I am scared that one day I will push myself too hard
I am trying my best
I feel pressured to do everything for my parents to be proud
I am there for everyone but no one is there for me.
I am honest and kind, but I struggle inside
I am full with emotions that I can't let out
I am afraid of what others think of me
I'm tired
I am this. I am that. I can never be myself.

Grace Williams (13)
Llangatwg Community School, Cadoxton

Autumn

As the leaves turn gold and crimson bright,
Autumn whispers softly, a gentle delight.
Cold breezes dance through the amber trees,
Carrying a scent of autumn breeze.
Fields once vibrant, now a patchwork quilt,
Nature prepares for winter, with beauty inbuilt.
Pumpkin porches offer festive cheer,
While twilight descends, bringing stars near.
In the season of change, we gather and share,
Warmth from the heart, love fills the air.
With every crunch of a falling leaf,
Autumn's embrace brings a sense of relief.

Olivia Harris (12)
Llangatwg Community School, Cadoxton

To Be A Kid Again

I want to be a little kid again
I miss playing in the park
I miss being scared of the dark
I miss not caring about how I look
I want to be a little kid again.
I miss not overthinking everything
I miss the glowing light-up stars
I miss pretending to be sleeping just so my dad would carry
me out of the car
I want to be a little kid again.
I miss not being told I am wrong all the time
I miss singing nursery rhymes
I miss not stressing about tests
I want to be a little kid again.

Tilly Roach (12)
Llangatwg Community School, Cadoxton

Horse Riding

Horse riding's the best
until it's the worst.
Will I fall off?
Or will I not?
If I fall off, will I get back on?
Or will I not?
Will I be the best?
Or will I be the worst?
Will I be jumping metres by the time I'm fifteen?
Or will I be stuck jumping 60 cm for the rest of my life?
Will I keep riding?
Or will I not?
I love horse riding; it's the best.
But will I keep riding until I'm the best,
or will I give up long before that?

Gwen Hart (13)

Llangatwg Community School, Cadoxton

Behind The Screen

Behind the screen,
Nothing has been seen,
All coming towards you,
And nowhere to flee,
So many lies you can't see the contrast,
Maybe one day the truth will unfold at last,
Why is it happening now?
It never really happened in the past,
Someone has been broken,
Although nothing has been spoken,
If there were an easy way out,
Everyone would want that token,
Once social media reaches its peak and help there is to seek,
Only the truth I shall speak.

Lacey Jones (13)
Llangatwg Community School, Cadoxton

Nature

Nature is all around us
It's always there, watching as the leaves blow off the trees
as the wind howls
Kids play and run around through the cold but silent field by
the farm
The wind is silent, still even
The foggy and misty mountains can be seen from a mile
away
You look down at the grimy rubbish-filled streets
You look back at the huge mountains from a distance
Completely untouched, unlike the dark and dirty streets
Nature is beautiful and we need to take care of it.

Amelia Higgins (12)

Llangatwg Community School, Cadoxton

Fear

Fear is always there,
Always waiting around the next corner, ready to jump you,
Like the monster under your bed that eats your socks, just
to annoy you.

Everyone has a fear,
Maybe it's the dark, it may be going bald,
What I am trying to say is - fear is fear.

It will always be there, but you can talk to someone,
You can trust someone to help you,
It's okay to have fears but don't let them get in the way.

Lilly-Haf Church (11)

Llangatwg Community School, Cadoxton

Bikes

Riding a bike is so much fun
It is great to be in the sun
I really enjoy doing wheelies
While some play in their Heelys
We must remember to take care
And not be worried about our hair
Always wear safety gear
So our parents don't have to fear
We must not worry about a flat tyre or how many times
Our seat needs to be higher
Riding a bike is so much fun
It is great to do in the sun.

Evan Coleman (12)
Llangatwg Community School, Cadoxton

Eggs

Eggs are all different,
They may be an oval or a splatter but the thing is,
They are all the same.
They could be hard-boiled, an omelette, or a newly-hatched chick,
But they are all from the same egg.
They could be white-shelled, or peach-shelled or a century egg.
It could even be devilled.
All eggs are heavenly and are all diverse, and it's okay.

Catalin Lazar (11)

Llangatwg Community School, Cadoxton

Success

The road to success is steep and long,
Full of changes where you must be strong.
With each step forward, keep your vision clear,
Success is the destination, have no fear.
Embrace the struggles, learn from each fall,
Rise again, for success is a call.
Persevere with passion, let your dreams guide,
Success is earned, enjoy the ride!

Aaron Joseph Case (12)
Llangatwg Community School, Cadoxton

Art Is Me

Art is me,
Art is something that inspires me,
Art makes me happy,
Art is what brightens my day.
So I sat down at my desk,
Grabbed a pencil,
And started drawing Sonic.
It's been five minutes,
I have a drink,
"Only the base?"
And it happens again,
Aaaand again.

Noah Bradley (12)
Llangatwg Community School, Cadoxton

The Girl

I am the girl who is a girly girl,
I am the girl who loves clothes,
I am the girl who loves make-up,
I am the girl who loves dance,
I am the girl who loves netball,
I am the girl who loves shopping,
I am the girl who loves hanging out with friends and family,
I am your girl.

Reese O'Neale (12)

Llangatwg Community School, Cadoxton

Make-Up

M orning, night, all I do is blend
A ll these beauty companies should never end
K eeping money just to buy make-up
E very day I save up just for make-up

U sing products just to enhance my features
P lease do not tell me off teachers!

Florence Matthew (13)
Llangatwg Community School, Cadoxton

Boxing

Boxing is fun,
Boxing hurts sometimes, but it is good,
A good sport to get fit,
You can focus on yourself,
Get into fights and maybe be threatened after the night,
Boxing is hard work and can make you sweat a lot,
It can never be forgotten.

Adam Griffiths

Llangatwg Community School, Cadoxton

I Want People To Know

I want people to know
How far I want to go
Through the moon and the stars
And maybe even driving supercars
I really want people to know
How far I want to go
Ride in trains
Or fly in planes
Before I
Can't
Anymore.

Sophie Roderick (12)
Llangatwg Community School, Cadoxton

Fishing

Fishing
Fishing is an escape
Fishing is a helper
Fishing is a saviour
Fishing can be good, and fishing can be bad
Fishing can be easy, and fishing can be hard
But in the end, fishing is great.

Sonny Jon Phillips (12)

Llangatwg Community School, Cadoxton

Therapy

Music is my therapy,
Music is my therapy, all of the time,
I put on a smile, you will never see me cry,
Hurting on the inside while smiling on the outside,
All of my thoughts running through my mind.

Lexi Dale (12)
Llangatwg Community School, Cadoxton

McDonald's

McDonald's is the best!
Walk in, all I smell is salt.
Hearing that ping brings back memories.
The way the burger tastes.
The way the drinks taste.
The paper straws!

Mason Hughes (12)
Llangatwg Community School, Cadoxton

Droplets Of Dreams

I see them, silver tears
gleaming down the window
droplets of anguish, droplets of hope
balancing precariously on the window's edge

I see the light
reflected in the glistening
creating prisms of light
a glamour

but as I reach out to touch it,
it dissolves
melting away from my fingers
an illusion

so I stare
I count each silver droplet
I count each dream that falls from the sky
and lands in a plop, bleeding into the dirt

in one, I see flakes of light
plush opulence galore
I see silk, saffron and chiffon
a woman placed high on a pedestal

in another, I see a verdant green
a rush of blue, clear and fresh
full, full trees reaching their wooden arms to the sky

in another, I see a blend of colours
black, white, grey, all swirling and mixed
hand in hand, people walk
men and women, black and white

but my favourite is the smallest
a blooming heart
reaching out, touching
so significantly small

but it catches itself at the window
and becomes bigger and bigger
and collects more and more
suddenly, all the dreams are merged into one

I feel its glow, luminescent
despite the fact it reflects no light
and when I reach out and collect it
it stays plump and firm,

eventually, it seeps into my finger
vanishing into flesh and bone
and I hear the whispering course through my blood
a hidden meaning untold

and I wish
more than ever
that people would keep
their droplets of dreams.

Lara Robinson (13)

Parkstone Grammar School, Poole

Keep Trying

They don't understand.
It's not that I won't do it,
I can't do it!
It's not hard to get!
Listen to me!

They don't.
"You were fine last week."
"It's not that loud."
"Try it, you might like it!"
"Stop making such a fuss."

I try to speak
But I have no words.
I can't fit in
The world's smallest box.
I'm not perfect, typical
I will never be normal!

I start to cry
The teacher sends me out
Leaves me to 'calm down'
I'm *not* calm!
How can I be?

It's too bright,
Too loud,
Too crowded,

It feels wrong
They'll never get me.

So, you stop trying to be
'Normal'
And slowly it gets better
I peel off my label of
'Difficult' and replace it with
'Me'.

I find the words I was missing
I tell people!
They start to help me.
They don't always get it right, of course
But they try

And they keep trying
And you keep trying
To be you
Because the truth is,
Being yourself
Is so worth it.

Eliza Coyne (13)
Parkstone Grammar School, Poole

Is This Me?

W ho am I?
H ow do I think?
O r how do I move?

A m I brave?
M aybe scared?

I s this me? Questioning everything about me?

A lways listening to what?
L aughing at what?
L ying about what?

I s this me?

K indness?
N othing?
O r something?
W hispering quietly?

I s this me?
S ad or happy?

T iny or large?
H ot or cold?
A lly or enemy?
T ricky or easy?

I s this me?

A m I me?
M aybe I am me -

M ainly I am me,
E ventually I am me!

Abi Fehrenbach (11)

Parkstone Grammar School, Poole

Fix Me

The half shattered -
half whole visage of you.
Like the swish of a lake encompassing my heart,
the fragmented delicacy of a mirror.

But you must tear it down, hide it away,
for what is broken is not wanted -
despite its hand-crafted frame,
avert your eyes, dare not look back

despair will fasten its cool, cut claws
thick vines blooming from its stems,
for in my shimmer of sunlight, it shifts
until they are cut.

And the lake stills. Breathe.
The sun rises. Bask.
Allow spring to turn into a new leaf.

Jessica Waring (16)
Parkstone Grammar School, Poole

The Frame

There is a frame,
And everyone has to fit into it,
There are some people who are willing to stand outside that frame,
There are some people who are scared of that frame,
Pressured to fit in by the world surrounding them,
They are scared to stand outside that frame,
Even though they wish they could,
But they feel the need that they should fit in,
Fit into the frame,
To be like the others,
And never stand out.
Ever.

Jennifer Jenkins (12)
Parkstone Grammar School, Poole

The Real Me

The real me:
It haunts me,
Scares me.

Scratches inside,
Running wild.
In bursts
And strolls
And sprints.

Sometimes it lies,
Sometimes it smiles.
Sometimes it cries,
And sometimes it snarls.

This is the beast within me.
The real me.

The me I hide
Yet this is the real me
And this me shall stay and be seen.

Ava Chapman (12)
Parkstone Grammar School, Poole

I Remember

I remember,
On one of the darkest nights,
Where despair had consumed me,
I hopelessly wandered into the woods,
Filled with dread,
I hoped to find a way out.

I heard a sound,
The sound of the river,
These wonderful waters,
I could never forget them,
As the moonlight reflected on them,
I followed the path it had given me,
Because of this river,
I had found home.

Bryan Beloti Lobo
Sharples School, Bolton

Branding

Humans love categories
Countries, food groups, car models, genders
Multi-questionnaires for life

Humans love categories so much, in fact
We forge an iron for our skin
It becomes our brand, persona, mask

I felt drawn to sunflowers
The roots called my name and I answered
An iron imprint on the soul

A luminous yellow petal masquerade
Hide between the tall stalks
Stalk between the short seasons

Immersed in the green leaves, blue skies
Autumnal chill, wrapping roots
The metallic taste in mine, I loved it

These are my colours, my style, my aesthetic
This is how I dress, act, my looking glass
This is my branding, etched with eventual ink

I plan for permanence, I am no short-minded fool
The before, however bewitching
I was not always drawn to sunflowers

And if I weren't always drawn then what
Took me in before? What was my branding?
Did I not have one?

Who was I before? Maybe
I am not me, a young me
Like a chrysalis, the old was boiled

A dead technology, he forged something better
Is this better? It is something
Greater than, lesser than, how fun to inquire

What changed? The caterpillar evolved
They don't do that without reason
An evolutionary advantage, what's mine?

I don't know if this flower is my face
Or if this is my mask
Is there a difference?

John McGowan (16)
St Andrew's RC Secondary School, Glasgow

Fear Of A New Beginning

Harsh winds blow my way
The hourglass had to tip over sometime
I never welcomed the crash that follows

I feel the first few grains of sand shift
Moving like the churning of my gut and I shiver
The rain pours around us with an unfamiliar harshness
She's shouting, yelling, screaming in anguish for something
we could never have.

A longer wave breaches
Dragging more sand into the water
I struggle against the tide
The hourglass wavering with every step I take closer to her

My tears fall like the harsh grains of sand
The hourglass finally tips
The sands around me finally settle
The rain stops and the hourglass stands still again.

Alina Avelaoei (16)
St Andrew's RC Secondary School, Glasgow

Waiting In The Wings

The curtains suffocate me as I wait,
Against their eternal black, I stand out like a sore thumb.
The florals I wear paint me as a picture of calm,
I am anything but.

Words fumble in my head as I wait and wait and wait,
An applause echoes across the theatre, in my head.
I feel empty,
I feel full,
There is no place I'd rather be.

I step out and the light catches me,
I stare into the darkness, yet I know they're watching on,
waiting.
I open my mouth to speak and my heart beats in my head,
There is no place I'd rather be.

Cara Mullen (17)
St Andrew's RC Secondary School, Glasgow

Red Stains

Blood spilled and reigned over moss and stone,
Those who met acidic salt, running across their flesh,
Which was scarred and torn from the penetration of
ammunition.
Bullets whizz past the ears of a toddler,
Whom trundled and wobbled past the corpse lining,
Tumbling over in a stack of Jenga.
The warmth of arms wrapped around camo,
Ripped apart by the separation of humanity -
Which would not be solved until the end of dawn.

Maja Nowak (15)
St Andrew's RC Secondary School, Glasgow

The Cardboard Box

The cardboard box,
Cold and empty,
The cardboard box,
Excited for use.

The cardboard box,
Getting off the shelf,
The cardboard box,
Heavy with food.

Driving in the car,
Sitting with my mum,
Entering the shop,
Holding all the food.

Putting you in the car,
Driving the long way home,
Taking away all the food,
Goodbye, cardboard box.

Lilah Pinchin (11)
Thomas Mills High School, Framlingham

My Truth

They asked me for my truth.
Here it is.
I am a day in midwinter,
Green jumpers and chai lattes.
I am the middle of the night,
Where I am hidden from the eyes of others.
When the dark surrounds,
It protects
From anything wishing to do harm.

I am younger than my future,
Older than my past.
This future of mine is unknowable,
My past, no longer within my reach,
Both unchangeable.
Unchangeable
Because I am sick of second-guessing
Every single choice I make
So, my destiny will continue
No matter the path I take.

My hair is bobbed
Like the suffragettes' was,
I would join them if I could
Because although I am short, I know where I stand.
I am taller than my worst mistakes
Because I know that redemption is always possible.

Sometimes I think I hear
Melodies not yet written.
They sing of peace and harmony.
And I try to capture them, but they keep
Fading out before I can write them down.
Fading out like a distant memory.

My eyes are grey, the colour of steel,
Ringed with honey gold,
And in another light, they appear
Blue like cornflower, green like the sea.
They are wide and always ready to learn.
The more I learn, the more I hate
The world we are living in.
Why can't we break the barriers, the divisions,
See what lies beyond our skin?

You can burn me down,
Try to silence me,
But just know that I'll return.
My other name is Phoenix,
I'll rise from the ashes.
This time I'm the one who lit the fire,
Ready to watch it all burn.

Emily Sheen (15)
Thomas Mills High School, Framlingham

I Am?

I am shorter than the memories I make,
They label me more than what I am,
I am taller than the story I started long ago,
I am sick of what I am not,
I long for others' happiness,
I am younger than my life,
I am older than the emptiness that left me years ago,
That's the truth that has led me here.

Amelia Hawes (12)

Thomas Mills High School, Framlingham

Student

In whispered winds and twilight's hue,
The beautiful truth comes shining through.
Like morning light on dewdrop's face,
It dances softly, a warm embrace.

It weaves through shadows, bold and bright,
In the quiet corners, igniting the night.
With every heartbeat, every sigh,
It holds the weight of the world up high.

In laughter shared and tears that fall,
It binds us together, the thread of it all.
In nature's splendour, in love's sweet call,
The beautiful truth reminds us we're small.

Yet in that smallness, a vastness is found,
In the simple moments, where joy is unbound.
With each revelation, each glance we pursue,
We discover the magic in being true.

So let us embrace the beauty we see,
In the truth of our stories, wild and free.
For in every journey, both tender and tough,
Lies the beautiful truth - our hearts, enough.

Archie Clifford (14)
Wexham School, Slough

The Great Truth

In the world of chaos and noise,
There lies a beautiful truth,
Hidden beneath the surface,
Waiting to be discovered by the enlightened few.

It is a truth so pure,
It shimmers like a diamond in the rough,
A beacon of light in a sea of darkness,
Guiding us towards the path of righteousness.

The beautiful truth tells us
That love conquers all,
That kindness is the greatest gift,
And that peace is the ultimate goal.

It whispers to us in the wind,
Sings to us in the songs of birds,
And dances around us in the laughter of children,
Reminding us of the beauty that surrounds us.

It tells us that we are all connected,
That we are all part of something greater,
And that our actions have consequences,
For better or for worse.

The beautiful truth teaches us
To be grateful for what we have,
To cherish each moment,
And to find joy in the simple things.

It shows us that life is a precious gift,
To be treasured and safeguarded,
And that we must do our part
To protect and preserve the beauty of the world.

The beautiful truth reveals itself
In the kindness of strangers,
In the generosity of friends,
And in the unconditional love of family.

It is in the colours of the sunset,
In the scent of a blooming rose,
And in the taste of ripe, juicy fruit,
That we find the essence of true beauty.

The beautiful truth is a reminder
That we are all interconnected,
That our actions have repercussions,
And that we must strive to be our best selves.

It tells us to be mindful of our words,
To be compassionate in our deeds,
And to be grateful for the blessings that we have,
For they are not guaranteed to last forever.

The beautiful truth is a beacon of hope,
A guiding light in a world of darkness,
A reminder that we are all part of something greater,
And that together, we can create a more beautiful world.

So let us embrace the beautiful truth,
Let us live our lives with love and compassion,
And let us strive to make the world
A more beautiful place for all.

Alesha Samiullah (11)
Wexham School, Slough

What Matters

In the stillness, I find my grace,
A warm cup cradled, a sacred space,
Laughter shared, a heartbeat's song,
In these simple moments, I truly belong.
The whispering leaves, the canvas of sky,
Remind me to dream, to stretch and to fly,
Each heartbeat tells a story, rich and deep,
In life's tapestry, love is what we keep.
Chasing sunsets, igniting the night,
Finding joy in shadows, in flickers of light,
A friend's warm gaze, a stranger's smile,
These threads of connection make the journey worthwhile.
What matters is not just the road we roam,
But the memories woven, the feelings of home,
In every challenge, in every strife,
Resilience blooms, giving breath to life.
So here's to the moments that shape who we are,
To hopes that illuminate, to dreams that soar far,
For in this vast world, what truly holds weight,
Are the loves we nurture, the hearts we create.

Zara Ahmed (15)

Wexham School, Slough

Transition To Year 7

I tried really hard but still not hard enough,
They think I'm really clever and look all tough,
I passed my 11+ so I look very clever,
But I can't be bothered, not now, not ever.

Then I end up in the local down the road,
But here it's a totally different ballgame, they just give you a load
Of homework and want you to do it before it gets overdue,
I don't really care, I just thought, *whatever, phew!*
But I can't be bothered, not now not ever.

I find maths boring and science even more,
I like art and English, but oh, drama on the floor,
Tech's good fun, but I can't seem to not get hurt,
I didn't finish my puzzle and came home with a ripped shirt,
I keep losing all my things, my mum keeps saying,
she's had enough but I just keep playing,
But I can't be bothered, not now, not ever.

I do need to go to school, and I do have some good friends,
But I need to work harder and try to make amends,
I know I am clever and I can do it with ease,
But I am the youngest so I do need to please,
I can do the work when I put my head to it,
In ten minutes sharp I've completed the real grit,
But I can't be bothered, not now, not ever.

I will try to change and focus at school,
Go back and retrace my steps and not be a fool,
I know I am a bright boy who can do well if I work hard,
I will try, I promise with a goal and ambition
You never know, might get a job in the Shard!

Yusuf Saghir (11)

Wexham School, Slough

Dancing On Ashes, A Celebration Of Survival

In the cradle of dawn, where the sun once gleamed,
Now only shadows dance on dreams once dreamed.
A lullaby lost in a wind that wails,
Echoes of cries, where hope once sailed.

Hands too small to carry the weight of skies,
Eyes too young to understand goodbyes.
Yet, beneath the rubble, soft hearts beat,
In a land where soil and sorrow meet.

Houses crumble, but love stands tall,
Even when the stars refuse to fall.
They build with whispers, stitch wounds with song,
As though tomorrow could still belong.

The earth remembers every tear, every stone,
Every child who felt alone.
Silent prayers pressed to shattered walls,
Where every step a shadow calls.

Ashes in the air like broken wings,
No more lullabies for the heart that sings.
Still, they dream, on the quietest night,
Of a dawn untouched by the soldier's sight.

Through bullet-kissed skies and barbed-wire dreams,
A people lost in fractured seams.

But even in darkness, a flicker remains,
A hope reborn in the heart's refrains.

They plant their seeds in fields of strife,
Watered with tears, but full of life.
For in the roots, in every tear that falls,
Grows the story of a land that calls.

AbdulRafay Mohammed (16)
Wexham School, Slough

Your Dreams, Goals And Passion

In a world full of noise,
A world full of dreams,
What truth lies in you?
What is your truth?

A person who dares to be different,
Or maybe,
Someone who just likes being around people,
Who just gets you,
Your friends and family.

Are you that person?
Who hides their true self from the world?
Or are you someone,
Who expresses themselves,
In the wildest ways possible?
Or are you,
Someone that's in the middle?

What is your dream?
Your hopes and dreams,
For a bigger future,
For yourself, and maybe others.

Maybe it's a sports aspiration,
Or maybe it's a career,
You would like to have.

What are you passionate about?
A worldwide issue?
Or just your love of food?
No matter how big,
Or how small,
It's important.

Why?
Because it's yours,
And only yours.
Your dream is beautiful!
So ask yourself,
What is... your beautiful truth?

Tiana Bhattacharya (13)
Wexham School, Slough

How Could It Be A Secret?

How could it be a secret?
When everybody knows?
The secrets that you keep are
Hidden beneath your eyes.
The ones that you cry for,
Are the ones that make you lie.
The lie that sweeps the pieces
Of your tiny broken heart.

How could it be a secret?
When the blood is pouring out?
Behind the glove of your hand,
Is a rose that marks you out.

How could it be a secret?
When the time of death is now?
Are you struggling to breathe?
As your throat is crumbling in?

How could it be a secret?
When only you're alive?
The cries of your people,
Are embedded in your mind.

How could it be a secret?
When the terror in their eyes,
Never leaves your sight?

How could it be a secret?
When the flashing red and blue
Is chasing you for life?

If only you'd known
That the love that makes you feel dead,
Is the love that makes you feel alive.

Bida Kodakkadan (14)
Wexham School, Slough

Captivating Truth

Many poets have spoken of this,
That the truth is never-changing.
And I have only one I can think of,
The truth that was, is and always will be.

The truth that rolled out Heaven's scroll,
The truth that set the bounds of the sea,
The truth that poured out love in spate
When He gave His life for you and for me.

So this is my beautiful truth,
Or rather He
Truth whose love who can measure?
'Tis as boundless as the open sea.

I am the Way
The Truth and the Life, said He
Ye shall know the truth,
And the truth shall set you free.

I have known my truth, and He has set me free
Truth incarnate has ransomed me
Set my heart alight. Consumed me.

This is the truth I want to proclaim.
From the rooftops and to the miry clay

Out of which truth lifted me
And proclaimed liberty.
Captives free.

Jane Joel (15)
Wexham School, Slough

A Message To My Heroes

In the sky of life you are my guiding star
No matter where I wander, you are never far
You bring love with you and never break my heart
With your wisdom, love and care
You have shown me the right path
You have always been fair
You nurtured me right
You taught me what's wrong and right
You gave me time
Through the highs and the lows
Your strength and kindness always glows
You corrected me when I was wrong
You appreciated me when I was right
You never judged for who I am and will be
You never made me regret my decisions
You never made me feel alone
You did your best
You did great
You taught me new things
You listened to me when I was in need
You helped me when I was in need
You are the light that guided me through my life
Thank you Dad and Mum for all you do
My heroes, my friends, I love you!

Zainab Arsalan (11)
Wexham School, Slough

Panic Attack

It was ever so subtle
The familiar sense of anxiety
Purely a quirk
A feature of personality
And yet how they fell prey
To its tendency to lay quiet and linger
As the bite of emotions slowly extinguished the calm nature
of character
The soft meditative concepts lost
As the breath began to sharpen
Each shuddering inhale agony
The urge to seek escape made a struggle against shivering
limbs
Until they collapsed in on themselves
And crawling into a shelter's corner became apparent
The arms retreated inwards to cross upon the chest
To comfort the writhing organ pulsing within
Whilst the fresh tears came to sting the eyes and quench
the trembling lip
A moment of pure terror
Bred from concealed inner torment and trauma
And yet before it led to this scene
It was ever so subtle.

Erin Murphy (15)
Wexham School, Slough

Dream Come True

In fields where shadows stretch and sway,
A symphony of leather and clay,
Batsmen poised in the sun's warm glare,
Chasing dreams with every daring flare.

The bowler's run, a rhythmic grace,
A whisper of tension fills the space,
As willow meets the ball's fierce fight,
Echoes of battle ignite the night.

The crowd erupts, a thunderous cheer,
Hearts beat loud, as victory draws near,
In every wicket, in every run,
A tale of glory, a race hard-won.

Beneath the stars, the legends play,
In twilight's glow, they find their way,
With passion woven into each seam,
Cricket lives on, a nightless dream.

Sahil Iqbal (12)
Wexham School, Slough

The Beautiful Truth

People come and people go,
What matters is getting a humble, loyal, harmonious,
honest, and above all, trustworthy friend,
Some people leave you with a lesson,
Others leave you with a long-lasting expression,
Or feeling that does not leave you,
So learn how to make people leave a long-lasting
impression on you,
People also teach you lessons that you learn from,
It helps you with the next thing to do,
And teaches you how to relate to others,
People also teach you how to move on without others,
And how to depend solely on whatever you have,
And also learn how to be independent,
Choose your friends, but don't let your friends choose you.

Christel Adjei (12)
Wexham School, Slough

I Want To Be...

I want to be a surgeon,
Dosing people with nitroglycerin,
Whilst maintaining
The operation table to not consist of a stain.

I want to be a paramedic,
And treat someone diabetic,
Driving around in a brightly coloured ambulance,
And not allow patients to experience apocalypse.

A doctorate I'd like to achieve.
Through body parts I'd like to cleave.
With that, a pathologist can be agreed,
Though they do not take the lead.

A nurse I'd not like to be,
As I wouldn't like to treat a sprained knee.
In the medical field, I would like to work,
As I am not the one to hurt.

Oliwier Krol (11)
Wexham School, Slough

Past, Present And Future

In the past I wanted to be an artist
because I loved the different colours and the way the artists
used different techniques and forms.
Even at school,
I spent most of my break and lunch drawing,
trying to get better and better every day!

I now want to be a doctor
because I love helping people and making them smile.
I am also inspired by my family
because my mum has asthma and when she was in the
hospital,
I saw how the nurses treated and helped her.

Only God knows my future...
What could it be?

Safiyah-Nur Mahmood (12)
Wexham School, Slough

Fight

Fists may fly and tempers flare
Words like weapons fill the air
Anger rises, hearts grow cold
Stories told but never old
Clashing egos, pride at stake
A battle fought for goodness' sake
Seeking justice, righting wrong
The fight goes on the whole day long
Through trials faced and lessons learned
A spirit strong, forever burned
With courage bold, we rise and stand
United hearts across the land
So let us fight with all our might
For what is just and what is right
With love as guide and hope as shield
We'll face the storm and win the field.

Qaais Rashid (14)
Wexham School, Slough

Friendship In Competitors

Faster and faster
The wind gushing through
Hitting my helmet like a brick
Moving left and right
Up and down the hill
Moving left and right
Overtaking my competition
Left and right
Defending as if my life depends on it
Adrenaline darting head to toe
Exasperated that I was overtaken
Like racing behemoths on track
But buddies after
Despite everything
Going to eat as a gang
The breeze cooling us down
As if the race was a dream
How would I live without you?

Sanjay Chandran (13)
Wexham School, Slough

Are We A Dream?

The trees and the sky are high above.
The birds chirping,
it almost sounds like they say something.
The rainbow forming,
and aeroplanes waving above.
Is it just me?
All this I could see in a second.
Then, nothing there.
As it was,
just a dream,
could I be,
could we be a dream?
As we lean in for the answer,
do we fancy them or do we fancy us?
They, one by one, fall.
Am I,
are we,
a dream?

Jannat Mubashir (11)
Wexham School, Slough

Mom, Truth That Remains

She was a steady and tall oak
Deeply rooted in truth and love
Her branches, still my abode
Even though it's long after
She has returned to Earth.

Her thin soft lips curved into a smile
As if the truth of her love
Could no longer be contained
Even as her body grew fragile
And the storm of illness darkened her days
Her presence in my heart
Remained an unbreakable thread
Weaving every moment of my life.

Manha Fathima (14)
Wexham School, Slough

The Beautiful Truth

Truth is beauty as beauty is truth,
And that is found within and behind your eyes.
A window to the soul is more beautiful
And truthful than any missing shout.
In truth lies beauty. It is beauty wherein lies truth.

Truth is beauty. Beauty is truth.
And that is found within and behind your eyes.
We are imperfectly perfect just as we are.
Learning to be unbecoming of the fake ideology.
I love beautiful truth.

Franklina Adjei (11)
Wexham School, Slough

Half Term!

Yay! It's the half term,
No more early starts,
Wake up late,
Have fun all day,
And play a game of darts.

Work comes first,
So I'll do my best,
And complete the tasks set,
With an extra hour of sleep,
I hope to get lots of rest.

Before I know, I'll be back at school,
With all my kit, bag and books,
Running, rushing, bustling about,
Back to normal it looks.

Maryam Moffatt (11)
Wexham School, Slough

Change Is Supernatural

Babies grow in obedience,
But they change in defiance,
Youths smoke the nicotine,
The meat of brown bean.

Change is hard,
Like the sword of the crossguard,
Change is good,
Like a fruitful childhood.

Change is good for the world,
And charges us up like a cord,
It stirs our hope,
Like the word delivered by a pope.

Isaac Ifeanyi-Ukaeru (12)
Wexham School, Slough

Why I Worry

I could be an engineer in ICT, but I worry my actions will come back to bite me. I could be a world-time baller, but I worry I won't be a top goalscorer.
Why do I worry?
Why do I worry?
Why do I worry?
Why do I worry?
Roses are red, violets are blue.
If I worry too much, I won't think it through.

Binyameen Alyas (12)
Wexham School, Slough

The Beautiful Truth

Beauty is just like an attractive book
But real beauty is great ideas of truth
One truth is better than a hundred lies
Never deceives for any self-benefit
Inner beauty of a person is reliable anywhere
Love of such beauty is real
Reliable to live with and sure.

Sammar Fatima (13)
Wexham School, Slough

Family: The Only Thing I Need In The World

F riends who never let you down,

A nd never let you cry,

M ake you the best,

I mpossible to compare with the rest,

L ike a seed without any weeds,

Y ellow is the colour of good deeds.

Aroona Aamer (11)

Wexham School, Slough

Growing Up

I listened to him
He listened to me
Or so I thought
I ought to have known
We both aren't grown
Lies uncovered, lies uncovered
Tears on the floor, tears on the floor.

Natalie Muswati (15)

Wexham School, Slough

Joyful Days At School

In the hall, where laughter sings,
Friends unite with vibrant wings,
Books and games,
Laughter bright, every day is,
Pure delight.

Shabbar Abbas (11)
Wexham School, Slough

The Beautiful Truth

I sit on my chair,
as I see the sun slowly fall
'twas the autumn
when lots of beautiful leaves fall.

Vishnu Divvela (13)
Wexham School, Slough

Good Boy

He's such a good boy
This is my dog Buddy
He's always happy to see me
He is such a good boy
His first day he ran into a glass door
He is such a good boy
He climbed on the kitchen table and couldn't get down
He is such a good boy
He got stuck in the trampoline ladder
He is such a good boy
He hides all of the shoes around the house
He is such a good boy
He digs up my dad's favourite plants
He is such a good boy
He fell down a 2.5-metre hole and my dad had to rescue him
He is such a good boy
He ate all of my sister's chocolate birthday cake
He is such a good boy.

Bertie Gregory (12)
Wrotham School, Wrotham

Between Two Worlds

In the quiet corners of my heart
Where the shadows linger along
I find myself caught between two worlds
Where I know I don't belong
The laughter echoes,
Yet feels distant muffled by the walls that bind,
Each side a different story
Yet
Both of them are mine
I watch as moments slip away,
Like grains of sand through time,
Holidays shared with one hand,
While the other waits unseen
Unheard - no joyful chime.
Frustration burrows within me
A tempest I can't express.
Longing for the fractured pieces to fit,
To mend the fractured mess.
Yet
I know that reconciliation is a bittersweet refrain,
As two families exist,
But love remains the same.
So I write this poem in hopes of finding peace,
To bridge the gaps of difference
And let my heart release.
Each missed birthday,

Each unmade phone call.
Grows into a mounting weight,
A relentless reminder it's not just a circumstance
It's a heavy fate,
In these lines I seek clarity.
A pathway through pain,
Hoping one day, acceptance will help my soul regain,
Sense of belonging in a world that feels so torn,
Forging a connection despite the distance,
Despite the storm,
In the quiet of the night.
Two homes stretch apart,
Love stretched thin,
Yet hopeful,
Binds every broken heart.

Freya Hopkins (12)
Wrotham School, Wrotham

Unrequited Love

Unrequited love,
A love that one has for another,
But isn't reciprocated.

I watch him every day,
I watch the way his hair moves,
The way his jaw clicks.

The way his eyes look,
I watch the way he holds her,
I watch the way he looks at her.

Wishing? Wishing it was me,
Wishing he looked at me like that,
Wishing he held me like that.

But instead, do you know what I do?
I stand there. I stand far away,
Looking.

Wishing it was us,
From the day I saw him, I was convinced,
I was convinced we were made for each other.

But when he sees her, I don't exist,
He's never glanced at me,
He's never said, "Hi."

Even when I hold the door for him,
He can't utter a thank you,
When he's with her, his whole world is her.

She's the only thing he ever sees - the only thing that exists to him,
But he's what I get excited to see at school,
He's what I think about.

Imagine your happiness, not knowing that you exist,
But you can't imagine that because,
You haven't experienced that,
You haven't experienced how unrequited love feels.

Unrequited love,
A love that one has for another,
But isn't reciprocated.

Faridah Lawal (13)
Wrotham School, Wrotham

Men's Suicide

Men's mental health may not be great.
But they can be great,
They just need to be believed in.
One blackberry may be good,
But the next may be terrible,
They may be smiling on the outside,
But they have an unsolvable pain on the inside,
They want to cry but instead,
They choose to die.
Men's mental health,
In the shadows where silence dwells,
Men carry burdens - untold spells.
With stoic faces, they brave the day,
Yet inside, a huge storm sways.

Kian Pennell (12)
Wrotham School, Wrotham

The Unfair World

I feel the world is unfair
In the world, we are urged to be perfect
While we emerge into something we are not at all
We are no longer what we want to be
Just what others want us to be
It daunts us to be ourselves
So we bury ourselves
Deep, deep, down
We are fading away
We are afraid of showing ourselves
The world is not fair.

Maddie Santer (13)

Wrotham School, Wrotham

Our Foundation

The older generation
I have so much admiration
Their face tells a story of hope and glory
Of the past
Which they thought would last
I wish I could see into their mind
To see the beautiful memories I could find
Without them, we would not be here
That's why we must hold them dear
The beautiful generation is our foundation.

Amelia Burtenshaw (12)
Wrotham School, Wrotham

Great Britain

G reat
R oyalty
E arth
A mazing history
T errific

B ritain
R oyal Britannia
I nternational
T ea
A mbitious
I t's ambitious
N ational.

Zach Baker (13)

Wrotham School, Wrotham

YOUNG WRITERS INFORMATION

We hope you have enjoyed reading this book – and that you will continue to in the coming years.

If you're the parent or family member of an enthusiastic poet or story writer, do visit our website **www.youngwriters.co.uk/subscribe** and sign up to receive news, competitions, writing challenges and tips, activities and much, much more! There's lots to keep budding writers motivated!

If you would like to order further copies of this book, or any of our other titles, then please give us a call or order via your online account.

Young Writers
Remus House
Coltsfoot Drive
Peterborough
PE2 9BF
(01733) 890066
info@youngwriters.co.uk

**Join in the conversation!
Tips, news, giveaways and much more!**

YoungWritersUK   **YoungWritersCW**

youngwriterscw   **youngwriterscw**